FROM VINES TO VESSELS
A Vine Gatherer's Handbook
(Second Edition)

Identification
Collection
Preparation

by
Beryl Omega Lumpkin

Edited by
Linda Gayle Fioravanti

All baskets and photos by Beryl Lumpkin unless otherwise noted.

The Overmountain Press
JOHNSON CITY, TENNESSEE

ISBN 0-932807-25-9
Copyright © 1987 by Beryl Omega Lumpkin
Library of Congress Catalog Card Number: 86-082900
Printed in the United States of America

2 3 4 5 6 7 8 9 0

DEDICATION

Dedicated to my mother who introduced me to the beauties of nature and who always found beauty where others failed to see it.

ACKNOWLEDGEMENTS

I would like to thank Linda Gayle Fioravanti for her patience in editing this book and her constant encouragement.

Thanks to the people who read **From Vines To Vessels**, Book 1, and passed on suggestions for this edition.

Thanks to the following people who contributed photographs of their work to be included:

Jack Battle
Jerry Battle, Tampa, Florida
Nancy Braski, Oak Ridge, Tennessee
Sherry Hudson, Rogersville, Tennessee
Mary Morrison, Kingston Springs, Tennessee
Redbird Mission Crafts
Louise Stoddart, Knoxville, Tennessee

CONTENTS

THE VINE WEAVER'S SUPERMARKET!
VARIETY OF VINES: These vines were photographed in The Smoky Mountains of East Tennessee and include wisteria, two kinds of wild grapevines, honeysuckle, poison oak, Virginia Creeper and kudzu.

INTRODUCTION

Tread Gently, For All Nature is Dear to Us.

As an artist, I have always felt that we should take full advantage of the resources which nature provides for creating. As a child, growing up in the mountains of East Tennessee, I used polk berries to draw purple-hued sketches on rocks, and used flower petals to create paintings. My sister and I created elaborate costumes from giant leaves and twigs, and made what we called "grasshopper nests" from long weeds. It has always been a natural thing for most children to create with whatever materials are available to them in their surroundings. Since natural materials are available to all of us, we are most fortunate and should take every opportunity to experiment and make use of them.

Although this book is basically about gathering materials for weaving baskets, the same material may be used for other artistic endeavors such as wall hangings, place mats, coasters, rugs, hats, etc. The only limit you have in creating is your own imagination.

In every basket weaving class I teach, someone always asks, "Now that I can make a basket, how do I gather the materials and where do I start looking?"

I find that many people who are unfamiliar with the outdoors are reticent to venture into the wooded areas to look for vines and weaving materials. If they do locate materials, they are uncertain about how to gather and prepare them for use. If you carry this book with you and use it as a "handbook" and guide, it should make the job of identifying and gathering a little easier and possibly introduce you to a few new materials and ways to use them.

The following information is written as a step-by-step gathering guide. Although the materials which are mentioned can be found mostly in the Appalachian mountain areas, many of them grow in other areas of the country as well. The names of the vines vary from region to region, and some which I refer to by colloquial names of the East Tennessee area have other names in different parts of the country. Although I am familiar with vines from other locations (and there are many), I will limit the information to those with which I am most familiar. Hopefully, the photographs will help you to identify the same vines in your area of the country.

When you locate vines with which you are familiar, just follow these simple rules and you will discover many vines you can use for weaving:

1. Make sure the vines are not toxic.
2. Twist one around your hand to see if it breaks easily.
3. Let one dry out for at least two days to see of it will retain its shape and not become too brittle to work with.

You have only to step into your own front yard to find many materials that you can use in weaving, such as grass, cactus, pine needles and twigs. In your own home such items as house plants (ivy, ferns, etc.) and corn husks from your kitchen can be used. Look around and train your eye to spot flexible materials which remain strong when dried, for use in weaving.

When I began pursuing basket weaving several years ago, I read everything I could find, seeking information on how-to and what-with. I did find some information on the use of natural materials, but it was not as complete as I would have liked, so I found myself trying any and all materials that I thought could be woven. I stripped bark, boiled vines, braided grass and weeds, shredded corn husks, coiled pine needles and did anything else I could think to do with all the treasures I gathered. Sometimes materials crumbled in my hands, or I would weave something using wet materials, only to find great gaping holes when it dried out. Quite often I would get discouraged when a vine I considered perfect, broke. Hopefully, I can save you some of the same frustration.

Gradually the vines began to cooperate, mostly because I learned to be patient. I cannot promise everything you try will work out the first time or even the second time; but in time, as you learn to handle materials carefully and experiment at different stages of growth, you will get the results that you desire. The trial and error time is important and allows you to become acquainted more with nature and the materials you are working with. In time, it will become second nature to you to recognize the right type of vine for the weaving you wish to do.

In the next few chapters I would like to share with you some of the secrets I have learned in finding, preparing and using a variety of vines and natural materials.

When you are gathering your own vines, you will no doubt find many more materials than I mention in this book since the woods and fields have a bountiful supply of usable materials in all seasons. If you try a new material and it does not work for you, study it carefully. Look closely at the way it grows, and the physical composition (i.e., fibers, bark, pulp, etc.). Check during all the seasons to see what season you will find it most usable.

Gathering natural materials not only puts you in touch with your environment, but also helps you get out for a healthy walk in fresh air, and gives you a first hand lesson in nature. You will learn to truly "see" what you are looking at, because your eye will become the eye of the artist. You will begin to recognize trees, even in the winter without leaves, by the curve of their growth and the texture of their bark. You will learn to identify vines in the same manner. You will not only recognize their bark, but also the way they grow. Being able to identify trees and vines in this manner comes with time, practice and patience. Do not hurry yourself or be too eager for completed work. Each step along the way is rewarding in itself, and the fact that you have a finished basket or other work of art as an end result is only an added bonus.

The rewards of gathering natural materials are numerous, besides the obvious one of having a beautiful "original" work of art in the finished basket or creation. No two vines or plants grow the same; so even if you repeat the same design with materials you gather and prepare yourself, each new creation is unique.

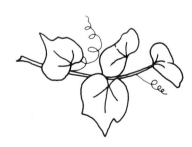

I

Gathering and Preparation of Vines

It is very important to have a proper respect for nature and the environment when gathering natural materials. Most vines can be gathered year round; however, fall, winter and early spring are the best times since there are no leaves and the vines are easily spotted. The summer has several obstacles. The heavy foliage can conceal snakes, poisonous insects, poison ivy and poison oak (common in central and eastern U.S.). It is not only more difficult to spot vines in the summer, but once spotted it is also more difficult to get to them.

When gathering, always be aware of where you are stepping when reaching for a vine. Some vines have grown densely for many years making nice hiding places for snakes, as well as homes for the more desirable creatures such as rabbits, ground squirrels, etc. Many birds also build their nests in dense vines and should not be disturbed.

A word of caution...always watch carefully for poison ivy and poison oak. Familiarize yourself with these vines in the summer when leaves are on the vines, and in the winter when the vines are bare. Both vines can be mistaken for such vines as Virginia Creeper and can cause great discomfort for those who are allergic to them. Both vines can cause a rash with blisters and can spread rapidly. I found out the difference in these vines from a bad experience. I gathered vines in the late winter, thinking I had cut Virginia Creeper. I started weaving a basket with them, only to find out half way through that the vines were poison oak! The basket frame still hangs in a tree in my yard to remind me to be more careful. Both poison oak and poison ivy have three leaves (see photographs). They can be found growing along the ground, fence rows, bushes and trees and other areas where vines are prevalent. They also grow intermingled with other vines. In early autumn the poison oak leaves turn golden and the poison ivy turns a brilliant red. The poison ivy has red berries in the winter. The following photographs* should be of some help in identification.

*I-1 (Poison Ivy) and I-2 (Poison Oak)

I-1

POISON IVY: This vine can be found creeping along the ground, growing in trees and low plants or crawling along a tree trunk. The plant has three shiny leaves which turn red in autumn. It bears beautiful red berries and should always be avoided. Like poison oak, it also can be mistaken for Virginia Creeper.

I-2

POISON OAK: This is what you *do not* touch or gather. It is very pretty at a distance and in autumn the leaves turn to a brilliant golden color. When the leaves are gone, the vine closely resembles Virginia Creeper because of the many roots which hold it onto a plant or tree.

I-3

VIRGINIA CREEPER: A look-alike of poison ivy and poison oak because it grows in the same manner. It is a good vine for weaving and very decorative as it hangs from trees. Unfortunately, it grows in the same areas where poison ivy and poison oak grow and is difficult to tell apart from them, especially in the winter when there are no leaves. It is best, if you are not sure, to choose other vines over this one for weaving.

Some basic rules to follow when gathering are:

1. Never pick a vine with flowers or fruit on it.
2. Do not pick too many vines in one area (even in dense woods) leaving barren spaces.
3. Do not gather in Federal, State or local parks, wildlife areas or private property without permission.

A serious vine gatherer will always have a knife ready for use since vines are found everywhere. It is a good idea to wear gloves, if possible, for protection from the poison vines, thorns and grasses which cut unprotected hands. Gloves also give a better grip when pulling vines from trees.

The following instructions for cutting, preparing and storing vines holds true for most vines though there are exceptions which will be mentioned as each vine is described. The best criteria for choosing vines is to find ones long enough to work with, ones that feel good to the touch, and ones that do not break when wound around the fist. Following these guidelines, the choice of vines then becomes an individual matter of taste.

Once having spotted a vine you would like to cut, pick up one end of the vine and look along it as far as you can see to determine if it is long and straight enough to cut for use. Sometimes the runners are too short to bother with, but it is difficult to tell when they are intertwined.

Pay close attention to the texture of the vine. If it is pulpy and soft, it is mostly water which will evaporate leaving you with strings not worth weaving (young kudzu growth is a good example).

When you are checking vines to see if they are usable, bend the vine. If it breaks with a sharp sounding "snap", it is probably dead and not good for use or too young to have substance. Even though it is possible to break most vines, a knife will cut several at one time and the very thick ones, which cannot be broken, much easier.

If the vine has leaves, it is more convenient to strip it at this time. Simply hold the vine in your left hand by one end and let it run through your right hand, stripping off the leaves as it is pulled through. Although this can be done after boiling, there will be more room in the boiling pot if the vines have been stripped first.

When the vine is stripped of its leaves, wind it around your hand or in a coil as small as you can manage. After several coils are gathered, a vine can be run through the coils, tying them together. They can then be attached to a belt loop or carried over the back. This method is more convenient than carrying a bag to put them in. Also, you may not have gone out with the intention of gathering vines, but have found some you would like to cut and must carry them as easily as you can.

I-4
Grapevines that have been coiled and strung on another vine which makes an easy carrying handle.

At this time, while vines are still fresh, they can be woven (with great care since they may break easily). This will produce a natural, colorful, more textured basket. You may also strip some of the bark from the larger vines and use the bark as an alternate weaver or as decorations. Since the vines break easily in this stage, they cannot be used for more intricate weaving. However, for large, loosely woven baskets, they will work fine.

Boiling the vines from two to six hours (depending on the type of vines and the size) will produce more workable materials which can be stripped of the bark more easily. Once boiled, the vines become more flexible and stronger. A basket woven with vines which have been boiled is also more "finished" looking and less textured than the ones made from the freshly cut materials.

The easiest way to boil the vines is to coil them loosely and place them in a large pot with a stone or heavy object on top to keep them submerged and covered with water. After the first hour, check them every half hour or so for flexibility to determine how long they should be boiled. I usually prepare a large pot of vines and let them simmer on low heat over night. That way I am sure that they will be boiled sufficiently and I do not have to keep checking them.

After boiling, the vines should be stripped of bark and any leaves which are left. The bark will be quite soft and loose at this time and can be stripped by holding a heavy piece of cloth or plastic scrubber in the left hand, pulling the vine through with your right hand. After stripping, the next step is to trim off all the rough spots. If you are using young, smaller vines, this is no problem; however, the older vines which had runners will have knots where the runners were joined, and can be smoothed down easily with a small knife.

I-5
This is my "outside" workshop, used in the summer months. The vines hanging are dried and ready to use. Unfinished baskets are also hung here while the work is in progress. An ancient washtub serves as a boiling pot for the larger vines. Honeysuckle vines have been stripped and are ready for use, while the bark from them is being dried out to store for later use.

At this point the vines can be used as they are, dyed, or hung in the sun to bleach. Some vines dye more effectively than others. There are several techniques which can be used for dying. One of the most simple ways is to dye the vines as they are being boiled for the first time, by placing bark or nuts in the water. This does not produce an even or dark shade, but works when you can afford to take a chance on the results.

One of my favorite items to use for dye is black walnut shells. These can be dropped into the boiling water with the vines, boiled with the vines the second time after stripping, or boiled alone to make a dye for soaking the vines, until the desired color is attained. After boiling the nuts (or shells) for dye, discard the shells and strain the dye through a cloth to get rid of debris. These rules will help with shades:

1. Very light, uneven color - **Boil** nuts with vines when boiling for the first time.
2. Medium shade, even color - **Soak** vines in prepared dye.
3. Very dark, even color - **Boil** vines in prepared dye.

Some of the other natural items which can be used for dying are: onion skins, bark, berries and roots. A combination of vines boiled together will produce varying shades though you have no control of the final color results.

At this point, the vines can be stored for future use if you are not ready to use them. Before they are stored for any length of time, they should be thoroughly dried. If they are stored before they are completely dry, they will mildew and rot. One of the most convenient ways I have found to store vines is to use plastic garbage bags, tying them securely and hanging them from a nail. If you have a dry area, vines can be coiled or made into wreaths and hung on nails staggered on a wall. This will also keep them for long periods. If made into wreaths, they can be unwound at a later time for use or used as wreaths.

You now know the many possibilities for using fresh, unstripped, unboiled, dyed vines. You can create numerous patterns with these three variations. You are now ready to look for your materials and are limited only by your imagination.

HAPPY WEAVING

II

Grapevine

II-1

Location: Dense wooded areas. Found in treetops, fence rows, around tree trunks, and along the ground.

Gathering Time: Late autumn through winter.

There are many varieties of wild and cultivated grapevines in all parts of the country, all excellent for weaving. The beautiful colors of these vines, along with the curly sprouts, make them a natural favorite for weaving decorative and sturdy baskets.

Tame vines are readily accessible in domestic vineyards now found in many areas of the country. Simply cut the vines back in the autumn after the grapes have been gathered. Roll the vines into coils (or wreaths) for storage or use them immediately (boiled, stripped or natural). They are most flexible if woven when cut; however, they can be stored for an indefinite period and soaked for a day or so before weaving at a later time. If coiled into wreaths, they can be used as decorations while waiting to use them for weaving. When you are ready to use them, just unwind them.

Domestic grapevines are not quite as sturdy as the wild ones, so are easier to use when weaving round baskets rather than the melon-shaped basket; however, with a little patience and care, they can be used for more shapes. For more flexibility, boil the vines, and for smoother texture, strip the vines of bark.

Although domestic vines are easier to gather, I find it most fun and rewarding to work with wild vines. When walking through the woods, scan the trees overhead for grapevines that are twining through the branches and down the tree. Grapevines unlike honeysuckle which usually twines itself around the tree trunk, sometimes hang freely, after growing to certain lengths.

II-2

Sometimes grapevines also appear to be another tree trunk because they grow so large and seem to extend from the ground up instead of growing down from the trees.

II-3

Wild grapevines growing in the tree tops and hanging from trees.

II-4

The bark of the older grapevines has a shaggy appearance, almost growing in strips. If the vine is cut close to the ground and pulled, the rest of the vine can be pulled down from the tree. It is a good idea to stand clear when you do this to avoid being hit by falling debris brought down with the vines. It is best to try to get the older vines which are leafless since they are much stronger. These older vines are excellent for frames and handles. Since many large, beautiful vines are actually dead, it is a good idea before cutting them to try to bend one. If it cracks and breaks easily, it is dead and cannot be used. Again, DO NOT CUT VINES WITH GRAPES ON THEM.

As with the domestic vines, the wild vines can be stripped of leaves and woven when cut. If the bark is stripped, you will find a beautiful, smooth. rich brown or grayish-brown color underneath. The bark can be saved for decorating later. Small sandwich bags are excellent for storing the bark for indefinite periods.

Grapevines are very flexible and good not only for making frames on which to weave, but also for weaving the melon and round basket. Try working with several sizes and varieties or mix them for variety of texture and to find the ones you most enjoy. The wild muscadine vine turns to a deep red-brown color when dried. The color is retained over a long period of time. There are many varieties of grapevines in all parts of the country, varying in color and texture. Thick grapevines woven into large baskets make some of the most durable and usable baskets I have found. Some of the most beautiful in design are those shaped with grapevine ribs and handles, and woven with other vines. Remember "variety" is the most interesting password in vines.

II-5
Grapevine from East Tennessee

12

II-6
Wild muscadine vines found in North Carolina. Two long pieces made this 4′ round basket.

II-7
This **5′ × 2′** basket contains grapevine from central Florida, bittersweet from North Carolina and willow from Tennessee.

III

Honeysuckle

III-1

Location: Growing along ground, entwined in trees and bushes, growing on fence rows in woodland and domestic areas.

Gathering Time: All seasons.

A basket made from honeysuckle is one of the most beautiful of the natural vine baskets. The smooth texture of the vine when stripped of its bark is not only lovely to look at, but easy on the weaver's hands. The finished basket with its smooth bark is a pleasure to touch. There are many varieties of honeysuckle, but the vine can be handled much the same in all varieties.

Another good reason to use honeysuckle is its abundance. It can be found in many areas of the United States, not only in wooded areas, but along fences, in bushes, or twining itself around trees in back yards. Many people would welcome an offer to cut their honeysuckle since it is destructive to trees and fences. If left alone for a long period of time, it can kill a tree or bush by twining around and around it.

This vine announces its presence in the countryside in the early spring and summer by the heavy, sweet scent of the blooms. The blooms vary from ivory-white to pink and bloom in some areas until late autumn. In the winter, leaves remain on some vines, and dark berries can be spotted on some varieties.

III-2   III-3

Older honesuckle vines growing alongside young honeysuckle vines.

Honeysuckle vine is very strong and makes a sturdy basket which is a natural for utilitarian use. To get some idea of the strength of this vine, in some instances, you can see where the vines have actually cut into tree bark as it twined itself around the tree.

Although honeysuckle can be gathered the year round, late autumn to early spring is the best time for cutting the vines. During this time the vines are most visible and easily accessible. The smallest runners creep along the ground and are some of the longest single pieces you will find. These are good for the smaller baskets and for use as the vine (weaver) to tie the basket together when beginning a new basket. As suggested in the instructions for gathering (Chapter 1), you can follow the vine with your eye as far as you can see to determine if it is worth pulling. The older vines (larger), usually found hanging from trees, can be unbelievably long. These larger vines are especially good for handles, frames and spokes. When you spot a vine which looks as if it goes a long way into the branches of a tree, cut it loose from the bottom and start pulling it. Be careful as you pull. Sometimes the vine you are pulling can also bring everything else it is twined around crashing down on you.

These larger vines usually have stringy bark which is very good for use as an alternate weaver or decoration. The bark will occasionally strip from the vine as it is pulled from the tree. Do not discard it, but roll it into a ball for future use. It does not have to be soaked to be used, and can be kept for a long period of time. The older vines have few, if any, leaves on them, and are whiter from being exposed to weather conditions.

III-4
HONEYSUCKLE VINES AND HONEYSUCKLE BARK.
**The bark has been stripped from the older vines and dried
for later use. It does not need to be resoaked for use.**

17

Please note that not all vines which appear "white" are worth gathering. Some of the prettiest of the larger vines, which are white from bleaching in the sun, are already dead and cannot be used. The inclination is to always take the white vines simply because they are white and beautiful. If you can break it with an easy snap, look inside to see if the vine has a solid core. If it is empty, then the vine is dead. Since you are already pulling vines from the tree, it is only a little added effort to pull the dead vines and discard them, for the sake of the tree.

III-5
Older, brittle honeysuckle vine and very young, green honeysuckle vine. Neither of these are good for weaving.

If the vines are woven immediately, there is no need for soaking or boiling; however, if saved until they are dried out, soaking them for a short time will restore flexibility. The soaking time needed will depend on the size and dryness of the vine.

Do not limit yourself to a specific size in vines. Although it is easier for the beginner to work with smaller vines, with progress you will find all sizes usable. It is a good idea to keep several size baskets going at the same time in order to use all of your materials.

When gathering honeysuckle, check the areas around your home. You may find enough vine choking a small bush or tree to make a basket and also be able to save a plant at the same time. I allow the honeysuckle to grow all year on my back fence. In the summer the perfume is always pleasant and the flowers are pretty to look at. In the fall, when I cut them back, I have plenty of vine to work with. The secret in this method is to cut them back every fall or they will get ahead of you.

When cutting the vines, choose those with skins that vary from light to dark reddish brown. Never cut the ones with green skins, as they are too young. When the skin is removed, the inside vine is greenish white. This changes to a buff color when boiled. If you choose to boil the vine, the longer the better for this vine. It can then be dyed or hung in the sun to bleach even more. Baskets made from honeysuckle which has been boiled lasts a very long time as evidenced from artifacts found, such as early Indian baskets.

When weaving with honeysuckle, try alternating boiled and unboiled vines. Use other materials as alternate weavers, for texture. The boiled, stripped vines which have been dyed can be alternately woven into the other combinations for variety as well.

When using natural dyes (bark, berries, roots, nuts, etc.) you will find varying shades of color depending on conditions of the dying, such as boiling the vines with the dye, letting them soak in the dye, and the condition of the vines when dyed. The boiled, stripped vines naturally dye more evenly than the fresh ones.

Now that you have several varieties of the same vine to work with, you can experiment with new designs or copy some of the old standard designs which have been left to us by our ancestors who found the basket to be one of their most useful household items.

III-6
Honeysuckle baskets made fron vines which have been boiled and stripped. The small basket on the right is made from natural, unstripped vines and cattails.

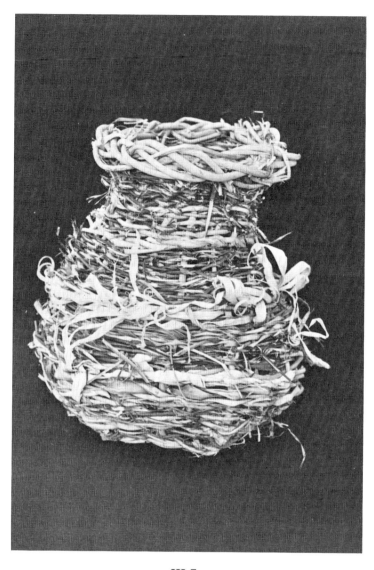

III-7
HONEYSUCKLE: (8″ wide × 14″ high) This vase-shaped basket was made from
fresh cut honeysuckle and trimmed with the bark from older vines. It is very sturdy
with varying colors of deep golden tones to white.

III-8

III-9

HONEYSUCKLE: (24″ wide × 36″ high) Made from freshly cut honeysuckle and trimmed with corn husks and pine cones. The top has a lip of approximately 2″. The basket is sturdy but lightweight.

21

III-10
HONEYSUCKLE: (2″ wide × 4″ high) This small basket was made from freshly cut honeysuckle. The roots and leaves were left intact, for texture. The top rim is laced with a small vine.

III-11
The basket on the right is made from boiled, stripped honeysuckle. The color in the center is from unstripped vine. The basket on the right is made from unstripped honeysuckle vines, cattails and willow.

IV

Kudzu

IV-1
Kudzu leaves and young runners. If you look closely you can see the hairy texture of the runners.

Location: Southeastern United States. It is found growing in trees or along the ground covering everything in its path including buildings.

Gathering Time: Late fall until early spring.

In speaking of kudzu, first let me apologize to those lovers of kudzu, whether you are a basket weaver or have a cow that loves to graze on it. I apologize for all the badmouthing I have done about this prolific vine. I have heard that nothing is all bad, and I have come to find out that this is also true for kudzu.

23

As many of you know, kudzu can be seen in the spring and summer months in the southeast covering much of the landscape along highways, mountain sides, and even in residential areas (Photo IV-2). If left unchecked, it can cover anything in its way in a short while. When I first tried weaving with it, I gathered the new runners that were green and hairy to the touch. I made a small basket and hated every minute of it because of the rough texture of the skin of the vine. I was surprised but relieved to find that it had turned into a lopsided pile of strings after a few days of drying out, and I used that as an excuse to stay away from it.

IV-2
Kudzu in East Tennessee. This area included several acres covered with kudzu.

I can now report a few good things about it. I did find that it is indeed usable for baskets, cows love it, and in the early autumn it produces beautiful purple flowers! The flowers are seldom seen because they are usually covered by the heavy foilage. I also understand it is eaten in some countries, and can be made into paper pulp. Its original use was for control of soil erosion. So with the combination of the above uses, I think we can look at it in a new, positive light.

A few years after my first attempt at weaving with kudzu, I had a request for a kudzu basket. I thought I would give it another chance and prove to myself that kudzu really can't be used. Much to my surprise, I found it to be an entirely different vine when gathered in the winter. I pulled the large vines which were hanging tangled and twisted together from a large tree. The bark was smoother than it had been in the summer, and had a beautiful grayish color. It had grown twisting and twining together creating beautifully shaped vines which could be used as handles. The first basket I made with these older vines was a pleasant surprise. The mature kudzu vines are more suitable for the larger baskets because they are tough and thicker than most vines. It is not as flexible as some, but is very strong and can be reworked easily without breaking. In fact, it cannot be broken. A knife must be used to cut it.

24

The negative side of using Kudzu is that the finished product does not retain original shape. When the moisture evaporates, the vines shrink, leaving spaces in the weaving and losing some of the original form, therefore a basket which starts out balanced may wind up unbalanced. It is lightweight when it is dried, and makes great outdoor baskets for planters. Of course the weather will eventually rot the materials if the basket is left outside any length of time. Kudzu is perfect for abstract shapes.

IV-3

KUDZU: **This photograph was taken in late summer and illustrates the way kudzu takes over an area quickly. This kudzu vine has grown during the summer months to cover a utility pole, a tree and now begins to creep along the power lines. The hillside behind it is completely covered. In the winter the kudzu will appear as lacework stretched across the hills and abandoned buildings.**

IV-4
Older kudzu vine. Good for weaving. Notice the way it has grown twisted together.

IV-5
KUDZU: A closeup of Kudzu creeping along the ground. These creepers are not good for weaving since they represent new growth and are full of moisture. If used, they will dry out quickly and feel like strings. They will not hold shape and will become brittle.

One undeniable fact, is that kudzu will always be in good supply. Even though development of much of our open spaces is happening everywhere, kudzu always finds a way to pop up and twine itself around something to grow rapidly. It is well worth your time to try at least one kudzu basket.

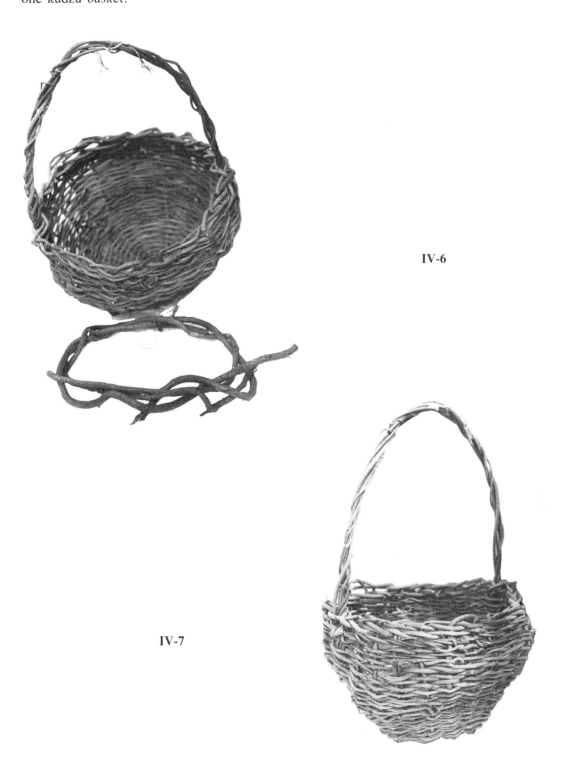

IV-6

IV-7

KUDZU: (24″ wide × 3′ high) This basket was made from kudzu which had been drying for several days after it was cut. As the water evaporated, the vines became hollow and lost their shape. What started out as a round basket became lopsided. The color is blue-gray and the basket is very sturdy though lightweight. The flexibility of its loose weave adds to its easy use.

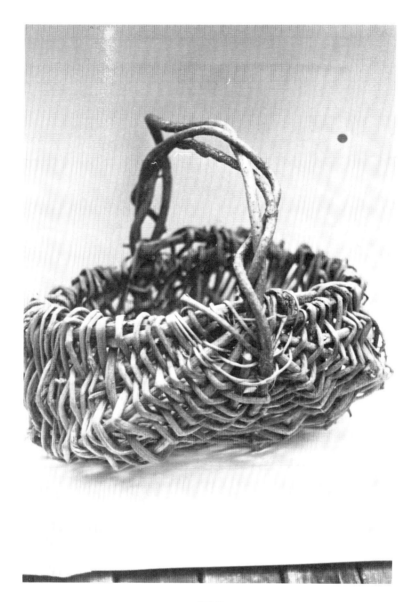

IV-8
Kudzu basket 2½′ × 2′ made from old, very tough vines.

28

IV-9
Kudzu basket 4′ opening, 5′ at bottom.

V

Willow

(Creek Willow and Weeping Willow)

V-1
Creek Willow

Location: In low, damp lands; along creek banks and rivers.

Gathering Time: Autumn to late winter.

V-2
Weeping Willow

Creek willow, also known as Black Willow in the Appalachian mountain areas, is a short, bushy tree with a feathery look. It grows along creek banks, in low lands which have moist ground, and where water stands. Quite often creek willow, weeping willow and cattails can be found growing in the same location. The bark of the creek willow is a golden, honey color and does not change after it is cut and has aged. It is most convenient to use the willow without stripping the bark; however, it can be stripped, revealing a whitish inside, which creates a smoother surface.

Creek willow should not be confused with the Weeping Willow. Both trees require large amounts of moisture and although they are found in the same areas, they look very different. The runners (branches and twigs) of the Weeping willow are longer and sweep the ground in a downward growth pattern. The creek willow is shorter, bushier and has branches that grow out and upward. The creek willow has a hardier appearance. The Weeping willow is initially easier to weave with because of the longer branches and its flexibility when first cut; however, it does not hold up as well since it becomes brittle very quickly. Weeping willow usually does not retain its color after being cut, as does the creek willow. In time, it turns from the golden tones to a blackish green color. It does, however, dry with a waxy finish, quite different from the creek willow, thus making it look as if it has been polished.

You should try at least one Weeping willow basket to get the feel of the difference in the willow textures. Once you have woven the Weeping willow, the finished basket should not be handled roughly because of its brittleness. This type of basket is more suitable for decorating than for utilitarian use.

The weeping willow is the first tree to be spotted throughout the countryside in the Appalachian Mountains in the spring. It is one of the earliest and most beautiful trees to have new, bright green leaves. This alone makes them inviting to weavers, but beware that the bees also spot them early and start swarming in them before the other trees have started filling out fully.

The use of creek willow in the early days of our country was as important for making furniture as it was for making baskets. Willow furniture is now making a comeback, and many modern day craftsmen can be seen working in the same manner their ancestors did to recreate the original designs, along with newer contemporary versions.

The most usuable creek willow is found in the new shoots which come up in the spring around the trunks of trees previously cut down. Those who are lucky enough to own a "stand" of willow regularly cut down the small trees in order to allow the new shoots to come up each spring. Although the shoots are long and flexible and are best for weaving, the creek willow twigs also work nicely for baskets.

The best gathering time for willow shoots is in the very late winter to early spring; however, the best time for gathering willow twigs or branches is in the autumn when the leaves are completely off the trees. The twigs break off easily and do not require cutting. They remain flexible for several days and can be woven easily during that time. Since these trees need lots of water, they naturally dry out faster than some other natural materials. They cannot be soaked and used, as some other materials such as vines, after a long period of drying out. If saved for a few days, they can be soaked and usually used with some flexibility. While working with them, they can be placed in a bucket of water vertically, to soak up the water or tied in a bundle and anchored in a stream or any nearby water source.

You must remember when cutting willow in the early spring, that the tree is in a growing state and does not stop growing immediately when cut. When the leaves are ready to bud, they will continue to grow for a few days after being cut. You may wind up with a basket full of leaves. This has happened to me several times. I was surprised the first time, but did it on purpose after that for the interesting effect created by the new buds. The first time I started weaving a willow basket, I left it half finished in a bucket of water in the warm sunshine. Much to my surprise, the next morning I had a beautifully budding basket. I thought it was so pretty, I left it that way. Of course, the leaves eventually dried and curled up, but for a time, I enjoyed a "living" basket.

V-3
Creek Willow switches ready to be stripped of leaves.

33

If twigs and branches are gathered in the summer, the leaves should be stripped, the twigs or branches tied into bundles and placed in a bucket of water. They will absorb the water and can be worked with for several days.

Willow, combined with stripped honeysuckle vines creates a beautiful contrast in weaving. The willow can be used in most any design and is one of the most durable of materials.

V-4

The short bushy tree in front is Creek Willow. The tree in the background is Weeping Willow. They often grow close together.

V-5
Creek Willow and honeysuckle basket in progress. This basket includes twigs
gathered during the four seasons.

V-6
CREEK WILLOW: (1½″ wide × 8″ high)
This little basket was made from creek willow
twigs which were twisted as they were woven.
The final look is a lopsided, cork screw vase.
It is a deep honey color.

V-7
Small 2′ round basket made from Creek
Willow twigs.

V-8
Creek Willow and honeysuckle (14″ wide ×
16″ high). Small basket is 2″ diameter.

V-9

WEEPING WILLOW: **(12″ wide × 10″ high) This basket, with a lid, is made entirely of weeping willow. The willow was used when it was first cut. This is a very basic "round" basket and can easily be made by weavers who are first learning to use natural materials. It has remained a deep honey gold color for over a year.**

VI
Wisteria

Location: In wooded areas and in residential areas where it is used in landscaping.

Gathering Time: Autumn and winter.

VI-1
WISTERIA (and bugle vine)

The larger, dark vine on top is wisteria. It is often confused with the smaller, lighter vine on the bottom, referred to as "bugle vine" in the East Tennessee area. Both vines can be found in many areas of the southeast. Wisteria has purple to white blooms while the bugle vine has bugle-shaped, orange flowers. The bugle vine is too brittle for weaving, while the wisteria vine is very strong and versatile.

Wisteria can be found from Maryland to Florida, and from Tennessee to Illinois. It is another wonderful vine which can be used in many ways since it is not only durable but flexible. At first glance it looks very much like kudzu (growing tangled from trees and twisted around other growth) or bittersweet (twisted in the same manner). Wisteria can be found in the wild, in dense woods, on old trees, and anywhere other vines find compatible growth conditions. Unlike kudzu and bittersweet, wisteria is also cultivated for domestic use. It can be seen in southern states hanging from arbors, growing around tree trunks, and decorating fences. It produces lavender or white flowers in the spring and decorates with its foliage throughout the summer. The twisted sculpture of the barren vines in the winter is also beautiful.

It is best to use this vine immediately after cutting it, or at least within a few days. Like kudzu, it does not work as well after it has lost alot of moisture, but unlike kudzu it does not dry out as fast. It is more friendly to the touch, not having the rough texture of kudzu. The dried color is not as pretty as the grayish kudzu or the honey golden bittersweet.

The wisteria plant can be toxic, with the foilage causing a rash when touched. The seeds are always very toxic. It is best to keep the plant and the seeds out of reach of children. Baskets made from wisteria should offer no threat after they are dried. This vine is best suited for larger baskets, or abstract vine sculpture.

VI-2
Wisteria Basket by Louise Stoddart, Knoxville, TN

VI-3
These trees are covered in wisteria, growing wild.

VII

Miscellaneous Vines

VII-1
MIXED VINES: These mixed vines have been twined together to form a wreath. Seed pods, berries and leaves have been left intact for decoration. Vines saved in this manner, can be used at a later date for weaving.

VII-2
Bittersweet Leaves

VII-3
Bittersweet Vine
The bark has a dotted texture.

Location: Mountain Areas, in dense wooded areas, sunny hillsides, entwined in trees and growing on trees.

Gathering Time: Anytime, though late fall and winter are best.

Bittersweet can be found mostly in mountain areas in dense, overgrowth. It can be easily spotted in the autumn by its bright orange and yellow seed pods. It is cut at this time by many for decorations and flower arrangements.

The bark of the vine is golden brown with white specs. If this is stripped away, you will find a stringy, silky looking interior. This fibrous interior makes the vine very strong and impossible to break. It must always be cut instead of broken when gathered. This same toughness makes it a sturdy and flexible vine for weaving. It is one of the best vines I have ever found to work with because it is so flexible, and will stay that way for a very long time after being cut. It keeps well and can be used for some time after being dried.

Bittersweet grows somewhat like kudzu and wisteria, twisting and twining around its host or itself. This creates beautiful shapes as the vines grow older. These twisted vines make wonderful handles and can be used for some very creative basket shapes. The younger vines are best for weaving but the older ones can be used for frames and handles.

VII-4
Bittersweet Basket

VII-5
Wild roses and other brambles in winter.

VII-6
Wild rose vine.

Location: Open fields, overgrown wooded areas, along country roads and hillsides.

Gathering Time: Late winter.

When you see the above vines growing, the first thing you may think is ''thorns.'' When you can see past the thorns, these bramble bushes have beautifully flexible vines which can be used, if handled with care. If you use gloves, you can cut and strip the vines of their thorns in the late winter before they have started new budding and the thorns are still pliable.

The skin of the wild rose is a beautiful ruby-red color this time of year and the raspberry is almost white with a shade of lavender showing through. You can see what wide variations could be created with these unusual colors. These vines are more suited for large loosely woven baskets. You probably would not use this type of vine very often, but it would be worth your time to try at least one.

VII-7
Blackberry bushes in summer.

47

WILD STRAWBERRY RUNNERS

VII-8

The strawberry plant above has runners extending to a new plant, and then one extending beyond it to another new plant.

Location: Mountain meadows, back yards, sunny spots in open fields.

Gathering Time: Spring and Summer.

The runners, which are sent out from wild strawberry plants to form new plants, are easily located early in the spring because of their bright red color. As the season matures, they start to turn a deeper red and then a dark brown. After the growing season is in full swing, it is harder to locate the runners because they are usually covered by tall grass and weeds. If you brush aside the leaves in a field in the winter, no doubt you will find a wild strawberry plant or two.

When you locate a plant with shoots sent out to root another plant, pinch the runners off close to the plants on each end, being careful not to uproot the plants. If you pull the runner, the plant (or plants) will uproot easily. If this happens, simply push it back into the soil and tap the soil in around it.

These little runners, small as they may be, are very strong and flexible. After they are dried, they can be placed in airtight plastic bags and saved indefinitely. When you are ready to use them, just soak them for awhile and they will be as good as new. They are best suited for very small baskets because they become threadlike in size when they dry. Since they are so small it is best to weave them onto a frame made with another vine such as honeysuckle. A basket woven with these small vines will lose its shape after drying out, unless care is taken to form a strong base, or mix the weaving with other small vines.

VII-9

The basket on top in the photograph above was made from strawberry runners woven onto a frame made from willow twigs. The basket at bottom left was made from strawberry runners and honeysuckle. The strawberry runners at bottom left have been dried and stored for some time. They can be soaked when needed for weaving.

VII-10
English Ivy

Location: Growing on houses, as ground cover, on banks, trees, rocks and walls.

Gathering Time: Year round.

English Ivy is often overlooked because we are so used to seeing it as decorative ground cover. It is a sturdy, tough vine which is covered with roots that hold it to its host. It is very rough to the touch, and really doesn't feel great to weave. It does work well for large, loosely constructed baskets. It dries out very fast and cannot be saved for more than two days. After it is dry, it cannot be soaked for use. Since it is limited in this way, it is best to use it immediately. it immediately.

Baskets woven with English ivy are lightweight when dry. This vine works better if it is mixed with another stronger vine or material.

VII-11
Forsythia Leaves

FORSYTHIA

Location: Growing in yards as hedges, usually domesticated.

Gathering Time: Late summer through late winter.

    Forsythia grows profusely in the East Tennessee area where I live. It is the first plant to announce spring with its beautiful, bright yellow flowers. The bushes grow fast and will grow back completely by the following season if cut in the fall. The long runners, which hang to the ground, are excellent for use in large, loose baskets. Forsythia is plentiful and easy to work with. It is not quite as flexible as some other vines, but still very easy to use.

51

VII-12
Forsythia Bush

VIII

Other Natural Materials

VIII-1
DRIED MATERIALS: From left to right: black walnut stems, wild rose vine, sweet grass, grass, pine needles, corn husk, (bark strip at top), honeysuckle bark, and bittersweet.

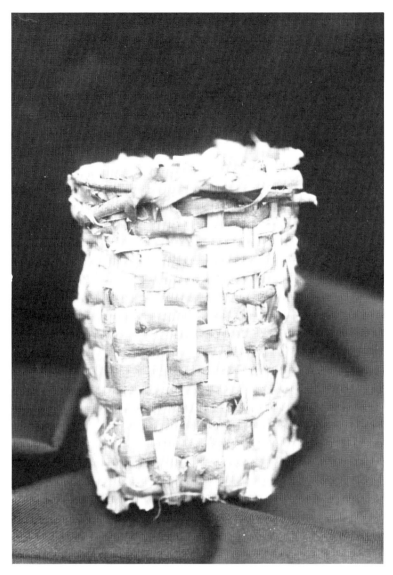

VIII-2
The outer bark appears dark, and the inner bark lighter, in this hickory bark basket.

BARK STRIPS: (4″ × 6″) The bark for this basket was made from small strips of hickory, stripped from a tree that had just been cut down. Small branches were stripped and the bark alternated from the outside of the bark to turning it to show the inside to form variety. The top is laced to secure the basket weave. This type of basket is best suited for square designs. Note: Do not strip living trees unless they are to be cut.

VIII-3
Black walnut tree in early autumn. The stems
can be gathered after the nuts fall.

VIII-4
BLACK WALNUT STEMS: Gathered in the Smoky Mountains in Tennessee. These black walnut stems were gathered in early autumn as the leaves began to dry and fall. When this happens, the stems also separate from the branches and fall with the leaves. As you can see they are 12-14″ long and make good weaving materials. As they dry, the color softens to a deep brown. They can be used when gathered or saved for long periods.

VIII-5
This very sturdy little basket, (5″ wide × 6″ high) is made entirely of black walnut stems.

VIII-6
Cattails in the summer.

CATTAILS

Location: Marshes, lowlands, ponds, and damp areas.

Gathering Time: From summer to late autumn.

Cattails can be cut while green and dried for later use. They are very decorative, and can be used as flower arrangements while you are waiting to weave them. They work best for square baskets, and are very light weight.

They can also be used in combination with other materials and as a finish border on round baskets.

Cattails can be used whole or cut into strips. They can be used in their natural light brown dried color, or bleached in a solution of clorox and water (about 1-5). Almost anywhere you find willow, you will also find cattails. This is a material to be experimented with, using them alone or with other materials to create designs, or to add texture.

57

VIII-7
Cattails. Found in lowlands and marshy areas.

VIII-8
CATTAILS AND GRASS:
1½″ × 4″. This small basket was made from dried cattail leaves and tall dried grass. Both grass and cattails had been dried for some time and resoaked for working.

CORN HUSKS

Location: All parts of the country where fresh corn is available.

Gathering Time: When you are ready to use the corn.

Corn husks are wonderful to work with no matter what you do with them. They can be separated from the corn in one piece, put in the sun to bleach out or just dried. They are tough and durable, dye beautifully, and can be saved indefinitely.

Corn husks should be dried before using. They have been used for making corn husk dolls in the Appalachian Mountains since the first settlers came to the area. This is a craft that is still going strong, and can be seen in most craft fairs in the mountain areas.

Before use, they can be shredded, coiled, curled or flattened. They arc resilient, and if you make a mistake with them, you can unwind them and use them over again without losing any of the material. Never throw away corn husks. Just store them until you can think of a good use for them.

VIII-9
CORNHUSKS. This material is used for basket decoration as well as in other crafts.

GRASSES

Location: Along roadsides, fields, untended lawns.

Gathering Time: Late summer, autumn and winter.

There are many types of grasses which grow in the above areas and turn golden in the autumn. They can be referred to as straw or just grass, but most types work the same way. They are most easily used in coiled baskets, but can be intertwined with other materials for texture.

One method I have found for using it is to start with a stem of grass and wrap the golden grass around and around it until it is covered. This can be coiled or used as a weaver.

VIII-10
GRASS GROWING BY A STREAM. This dark green, tubular shaped grass is excellent for weaving, coiling or intertwining with other materials and dries to a grayish green shade. The ends curl naturally, which creates a very decorative effect. (See photo VIII-14)

VIII-11

GRASS: (4″ wide × 3″ high.) This grass is found along creek and river banks and in low lying marshlands in the Southeast. It is a deep green when cut and very flexible. When it dries, it becomes a grayish-green color. It can be woven or coiled and curls naturally, making it easy to work with and finishes as a soft, flexible basket. (See photo VIII-10)

VIII-12
Grass from the lawn, used for intertwining with other basket materials.

VIII-13
A variety of grasses, all usable for different types of baskets.

VIII-14
Sweetgrass basket, woven with South Carolina sweetgrass and pine needles.

The low country basket weavers in South Carolina work with sweet grass and pine needles. This traditional way of weaving has been passed down through their families since the 1600's when slaves used baskets called "fanner" baskets, for cleaning grain. They brought this skill with them from West Africa and adapted it to the South Carolina area. They used sweet grass mixed with pine needles for added color and design, and coiled into baskets of varying shapes and sizes. Many booths still line a stretch of U.S. 17 near Charleston, where you can buy these sweet grass baskets. The basket weavers of South Carolina are proud of their skill and will take the time to show an interested visitor their craft.

PINE NEEDLES

Location: Mostly in southern states in wooded pine thickets.

Gathering Time: Year round.

The beautiful long pine needles found in the deep South offer quite a challenge, and are used very differently than the mountain vines. These needles are used in coiled baskets and are mixed with grasses as mentioned earlier (See Grasses). The pine needle baskets are woven in intricate designs using only pine needle construction. They can be laced with palm leaf strips or raffia. When the pine needles first fall from the tree they are very flexible, and can be gathered and stored for later use. The basket illustrated in this chapter is one of the most beautiful I have seen, and has many hours of work in the delicate ''stitching'' of the needles in the swirled design.

These pine needles can also be used as decorative additions to other baskets and creations combined with many other materials.

VIII-15

VIII-16

Pine needles are stitched with raffia, coiling them in a circular pattern to form an intricately designed basket.

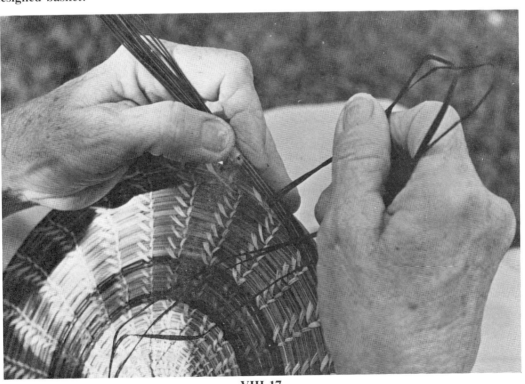

VIII-17

VIII-18

This basket, created by Jerry Battle of Tampa, Florida, is made from long pine needles which are found in many of the southern states. This is an excellent example of a "coiled" basket. The design is created by starting the coil from the center and alternating the stitches (made with raffia), which hold it together, as the coils are sewn together to form the basket shape.

VIII-19

HOUSE PLANTS

Location: In homes where plants are loved but keeper is forgetful.

Gathering Time: Before anyone sees that you have neglected them.

When your house plants die (as mine often do), they can be salvaged for weaving thus absolving some of the guilt while being creative. If you notice a fern without leaves, it looks like a string lacework. Since I have a special talent for killing ferns, they were my first domestic plants to weave into a basket. Although the basket was small, it turned out nicely. I found the tiny, fragile weavers best suited for a round basket, mixed with honeysuckle.

Various types of ivy can be used, along with large-leafed plants which can be rolled or stripped and woven. The best way to know what types you can use is to experiment.

The best rule to follow is to check the stem. If it is soft and pulpy, it is full of water and will dry up into a brittle, unusable material. If the plant is already dried out when you discover it, try soaking it for awhile to see if it becomes pliable.

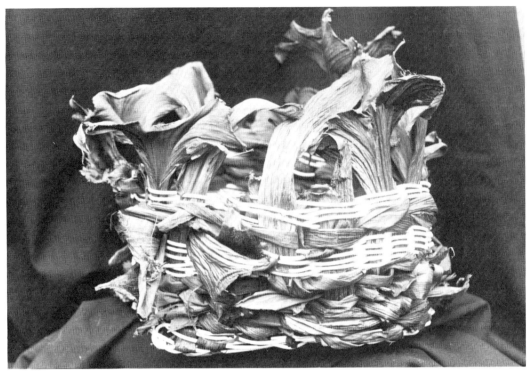

VIII-20

Basket made from split-philodendren leaf sheaths. These sheaths fall off the plant as the leaves unfold. They turn a copper color as they dry.

VIII-21
Bottom of basket.

VIII-22
FROM THE SHEATHS OF LEAVES OF A SPLIT-PHILODENDREN PLANT. Many large leaf house plants can be used to make the same type of basket. The leaves are laced together starting at the bottom and working up to form sides. Vines can be alternated to give strength to the shape. The ends are left sticking up around the top of the basket to give added design.

IX

Weaving The Basket

Some of you are experienced basket weavers, or have taken basket weaving lessons and feel very comfortable in weaving or constructing a new basket. If this is the case, you may feel these instructions are too elementary for you. This chapter is especially for those of you who have never tried to make a basket on your own, or for those who are working with natural materials new to you, and for those who know how to work with other materials but would like to feel comfortable with weaving vines.

The terminology used in this chapter for materials and techniques varies with individual weavers and different parts of the country, therefore, the terms and instructions which follow have the most simple explanations, using words which I find are most easily understood. These instructions are only a beginning to help you get started in weaving with vines. Hopefully your first efforts will resemble a basket and give you the incentive to continue trying new materials. After you learn these very basic principles, you can then proceed to more refined weaving techniques and materials.

Before we begin, put yourself in the right frame of mind by imagining that you have been walking through the woods and have gathered some wonderful grapevines and honeysuckle vines. You have stripped the vines of their leaves, and now you cannot wait until you get home to try your hand at weaving the vines. Then you find a nice shady spot and take stock of your materials. To complete the picture, imagine that the only tool you have with you is a knife (Good gatherers always carry a knife). You don't have string, breadwrapper ties, measuring tapes, wire, or any of the convenient tools often mentioned in basket weaving instructions.

Now there you are, just you, mother nature and a treasure of vines. The pioneer spirit rises up and you can see yourself as an Indian or pioneer living from the resources of the land. You will work with no **exact** measurements, taking full advantage of the flexibility of using vines instead of neat, commercially prepared materials. Now that you have put yourself in the right frame of mind and are filled with enthusiasm, you are ready to create.

For your first basket, you will start with a simple approach and make a basic basket. As I have mentioned, when most vines are first cut (See Chapter I - Gathering), they do not need to be soaked if they are to be used immediately, so it will be easier to work with them than with commercial materials which must first be soaked to make them more flexible. At this point, an important word to remember is "patience". The vines have been growing their own natural way, unhindered, and must be handled gently and slowly to form the shape you want. Your patience will pay off when you realize the slower you work at first, the less likely the vines are too snap. As you progress it will get easier, and you will work more rapidly as you become more familiar with handling each type of vine. OK...READY!

IX-1
Round basket made from creek willow twigs.

SIMPLE ROUND BASKET

We will start with a "round basket" because it is the most simple to begin with, when using fresh vines. This basket shape is easier than other shapes because the vines do not have to be bent sharply, and can be woven around gently without breaking. This design gives you more satisfaction, than a design that invites the vines to break continually. This can be so frustrating that many people give up when they first try, deciding that the vines are not any good. Do not be discouraged! If one vine breaks, try another, exercising more patience. Fresh vines (ones that have not been boiled or soaked) are more difficult, but the textures and uniqueness of fresh vines outweigh any inconvenience. It is fun and rewarding when you locate a vine and can work with it immediately.

We will begin with honeysuckle vines because they are more flexible than most vines, easier to work with when freshly cut, and accessible in most areas where vines are found. To begin the basket, first cut eight pieces of vine approximately the same size. (Since we are not using a measuring tape, try measuring from your fingertip to your elbow or if you don't like that idea, just cut eight pieces which look good to you). Try not to make them too long because it is more difficult to work with vines if the ends get in your way while weaving. Then cut a ninth piece of vine half the size of the other eight. You now have your spokes to weave onto.

To begin, cross four pieces of vine over another four, forming a cross. These will be referred to as "spokes". Now choose a very small, flexible piece of honeysuckle vine (hereafter referred to as the "weaver") and place it behind the cross from the top left-hand corner down to the right hand corner coming out between the center and the right-hand set of four vines (Photo IX-2). Wrap the vine backwards over the end of the weaver and the four pieces of vine and all the way around bringing it back toward you (Photo IX-3).

IX-2

IX-3

IX-4

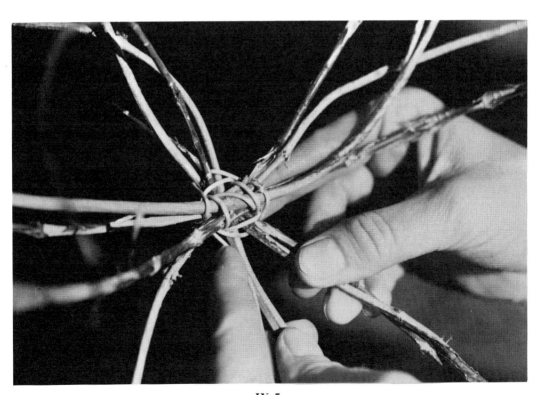

IX-5

74

Start to weave over **four** and under **four** vines at one time until you return to the spot where you started. At this point wrap the vine all the way around and start back in the opposite direction, weaving over **four** and under **four** until you once again return to the beginning (Photo IX-4). At this point, the cross is securely fastened together. Start weaving over **two** and under **two**, separating the spokes as you weave between them to start forming the appearance of a wheel (Photo IX-5). After you have woven around once, over and under two at a time, and have returned to the beginning, once again separate the spokes, completing the wheel effect as you weave around again, over and under **one** at a time.

When you return to the beginning you must insert the half piece of vine you cut in the beginning (Photo IX-6). To do this, simply insert it beside one of the other pieces in the spoke. This will give you 17 spokes to weave on to. You must remember to always have an uneven number when weaving or your weaving will not come out even. Now continue to weave over and under one at a time as far as you want to go until you get the basket bottom to the size you feel you want.

As you weave, instead of going around in a simple circle, draw you weaver vine up between the spokes and down over the next one, pushing it in close with your other hand. This creates a tighter weave. Use the hand most convenient for you to use to hold the basket. When you see your basket spokes begin to spread further apart, which will happen as the basket gets larger, you must add more spokes. When adding spokes, you should always add an even number or you will wind up with an even number. It is a good idea to always add the same number of spokes you already have, minus one. In other words if you add more spokes to the bottom at this point, you should add sixteen pieces of vines, therefore retaining an **uneven** number (33).

While weaving, you may change your pattern by adding a different type of vine, a different color, or weave two pieces of vine at a time instead of one. After you learn the basics of weaving you will realize there are many ways to change the pattern and texture, but we will not go into that here while you are sitting in the middle of the woods with limited supplies.

When your first weaver runs out, simply insert another one right before the first one ends, going in the same direction, so your weaving pattern will not be broken. Insert the end toward the other side of the weaving as you are looking at it. This will be the inside of your basket and you can clip all the loose ends from the inside when the basket is finished.

Now, let us say that you have woven the bottom to a size you like. If this is your first attempt at weaving it might be bowing on you and will not sit flat. To keep this from happening, alternately weave from one side to the other and as you do so, never "think" **basket**. This may sound funny, but if you are continually thinking that you want to make the basket into a bowl shape, then it starts to happen while you are working. (Just a little psychology to use on your basket to get ahead of the game.) The biggest reason your basket will not sit flat is that you may be pulling the weaver too tightly and this starts to bow the bottom prematurely. This often happens when you are too uptight or trying for perfection in your weaving. Just let it happen naturally and take control of the shape by tightening up later on when you are more familiar with your materials. To save face...if it bows anyway, just call it a "hanging basket". You might as well have fun while you are learning and turn your mistakes into "creations".

When you are ready to make the basket sides there are several ways of forming them. However, at this point you will be using the easiest method, and that is one of pulling the weaver tighter as you weave. The moment you start pulling the weaver tighter, your basket starts to bow and form sides. That is why you do not want to do it until you are through with the bottom. Now play close attention to what is happening to your basket sides. If you want the sides to create a round bowl effect, tighten up when you start up the sides. Loosen up some after about three times around and then tighten up again. As you weave, experiment to see how different tensions of weaving will alter the appearance of the shape of the basket. There are many materials you can find around you in the woods to add to your basket for variety, such as bark stripped from large vines; grasses; berries; pine cones; seed pods; various vines; twigs and anything else you find interesting. It is interesting to see how many different

IX-6
Inserting odd numbered spoke.

IX-7
The beginning of the bottom of a basket. The spokes have been separated to resemble a wheel.
Two sizes of honeysuckle and a small finished basket are shown at the bottom.

materials you can find to use in one spot without moving more than a foot away. You will be surprised when you really see what is around you.

Although there are easier ways to start weaving the sides of your basket, at this point, you are just learning to use the vines. At this time, the design and the weaving techniques are not the most important things. After you know how to handle the vines you can then experiment with various weaves.

IX-8
This is the beginning of a "round" basket made from kudzu. As you can see the bottom has started to bow and the spokes already form a "bowl" shape. Since the finished basket did not have a flat bottom and did not sit properly, it became one of many "hanging" baskets.

77

At this point you have learned how to keep the bottom flat, and how to make the sides of your basket. You can finish it in several ways. If you would like to add a handle, the easiest way is the way I first did it, and that was to choose a larger piece of vine than the ones in the basket and stick it as far down in one side as I could, and then extend it to the other side and insert it beside another spoke.

If you want to be a little bit more controlled in your planning, leave one spoke longer than the others and insert it into the opposite side when the basket is finished. You can then insert a new piece of vine at the same place you are inserting the end of the long handle piece. Wrap it back to the other side around and around the handle and stick it in beside the handle spoke on the other side. This creates a stronger handle and a somewhat more finished look.

IX-9

Finishing the Top — Step I.
Weave one spoke behind the one to the right and out to the front.

IX-10

Step II.
Take the spoke over the one to the right and stick it to the inside of the basket. Repeat steps I & II until finished.

If you hold your basket up now you will see all the ends of the spokes sticking up. One easy way to finish the top is to cut the tops off even all the way around. Hold several pieces of vine, flat piece of bark or cattail against the outside edge forming a rim and lace around it as if you are sewing to hold it in place.

The next way to finish off your basket sounds more complicated, but after a few attempts, it will be easy. As all the spoke ends stand up from your basket take one end behind the one to the right and put it out again. Then go to the one to the right (which is still sticking up), put it behind the next one and pull it forward, working all the way around the basket in this manner. After you have pulled about three spokes forward, they will start to stay in place. When you return to the beginning, take a spoke which you pulled forward from behind, and is now sticking out to the outside, and put it over the one to the right pushing it inside the basket rim, doing this all the way around. This will secure the basket rim and keep the rest of the basket locked in. After the pieces which are sticking out in the inside are trimmed, you will have a neat round basket.

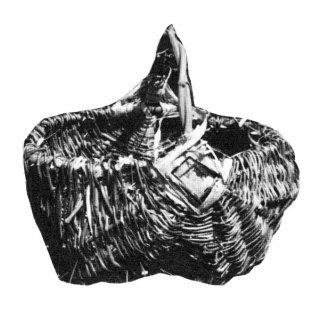

IX-11

MELON SHAPED BASKET AND VARIATIONS

Since grapevine is very sturdy, we will use it to form a melon-shaped (or some variation) frame for this basket. With this design, you will form a frame and weave onto it. Grapevine will be used for the rim, handles and ribs (the parts which form the frame).

To begin, choose a sturdy piece of vine of any length. If it makes you feel in more control, to be more precise, measure it the length of your arm and double it. The first thing you want to do is to make a sturdy handle which will be in the shape of a loop. To do this simply make a loop of the vine using about half of its length, wrapping the rest of the vine around that loop until it stays together as one continuous loop. Next, make another the same way, but just a little smaller. If at first the ends of the vine do not stay together, keep rewrapping one end around and around the loop until it does stay in. Sometimes you will find you have to wrap it tighter than when you first started. Remember, you are only working with one piece of vine to create the loop.

Now that you have two loops, you can proceed with the frame of the basket. I have found that it is easier to put the larger loop inside the smaller one to help hold them together until they are secured. After some practice, you can try both ways. After you have positioned the two loops together, tie a small piece of vine around the top of one of the loops which will be considered your handle. By moving the loop which makes the rim from the middle, higher up on the handle or lower down from the middle, you will determine the depth of your basket. The rim can be moved up almost to the top of the handle which will result in a very deep basket. If it is moved down to the bottom, it will result in a shallow basket. Obviously, if the loop is placed in the middle of the other loop, you will have a more rounded basket. So much for experimenting at this stage.

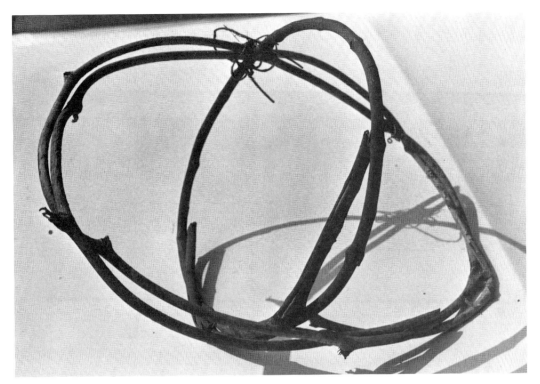

IX-12
The two circles of vines, one inside the other, forms the beginning of the frame.

The next step is to attach the two loops together on each side using a design shape referred to as the "God's eye". When you have decided where the two loops will intersect, make a small nick on the inside of the handle and the outside of the rim so they will fit more neatly where they intersect. (Remember you do have a knife to work with).

Looking at the spot where the two loops join, imagine two sticks forming a cross. Some of you may remember doing this with popsickle sticks when you were in the scouts. before you begin, cut two pieces of **very** flexible honeysuckle vine (easier to use than grapevine as a weaver), both the same size, at least as long as your arm (a primitive measuring stick). Looking at the cross, insert one end of the vine behind the two hoops from the bottom right up to the top left-hand corner. Bring the vine over the front of the cross to the bottom right-hand side between the end of the vine and the bottom of the cross (Photo IX-12). Now move it behind the right-hand rim (loop) and around it, over the top (Photo IX-13). Moving clockwise, cross over the top of the next loop, and all the way around it (Photo IX-14), over the top of it to the top of the next loop, all the way aound that one to the top of the next one, all the way around to the next one. Remember, you are traveling clock-wise and can establish a rhythm to your movement by turning the frame in your hand as you go, if you like, to make it easier. The "God's eye" will begin to form into a diamond shape (Photo IX-15).

IX-13

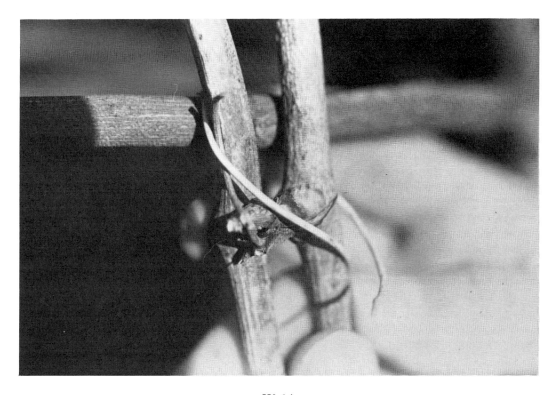

IX-14

IX-15

IX-16

One mistake many people make is to skip one part of the cross (or one side of the loop). If you do this, just unwind the "God's eye" to a point where it was correct and start over. Wrap the honeysuckle around and around each point of the cross, making sure it does not pile up on top of itself, but presents a flat diamond-shaped design. This is accomplished by laying the vine **beside** the previous piece as you wrap it. When you reach the end of the vine, tuck it securely through the side of the diamond to hold it until you weave over it. Add another piece to it by tucking the new piece in where the old one ended. Note, you will see the word "tuck" often in these instructions. It is one of the most helpful words you will come to know.

If you turn your basket over, you will see that the large vine which forms the bottom half of the loop divides the basket into two sections on the bottom. Always weave the same amount on each side, first one side and then the other to keep it balanced. Now it is time to move to the other side. Make sure your vine for securing the other side of the frame together is approximately the same length as the first one. If by some chance it was measured wrong, count the times it went around the other side. Since vines do not grow in a uniform size, it is easier to measure your diamond across the middle by using a piece of vine. This way you can make the "God's eyes" the same width on both sides. As you can see already, this type of instruction is very unscientific and unsystematic. It is explained this way on purpose to allow the weaver more flexibility with the vines. Unlike commercially prepared materials, no two vines are the same size or texture, so vine will not always turn out the same width in the design. You must learn, at an early stage, to compensate by adding or subtracting as you weave in order to get a somewhat uniform shape or design. The only thing that I feel is really important for a vine basket is that it sit up when finished. The more unusual it is, the more interesting it is. For those of you who want tranquility and uniformity in your work, you can achieve that by compensating with the vines as mentioned before.

In weaving a melon shaped basket, or a variation of this design, always remember that anything you add to one side you must also add to the other side. This is more for balance in design and shape than for perfection. Always cut two lengths of vine at the same time, one for each side. Always cut the ends at an angle or pointed.

Now, we are ready to add the ribs. I find it easier to add three, then two, then one at a time. The reason I add three to begin with is to achieve the shape at an early stage. You may vary this if you like since each basket you weave with vines will be different and have a unique design on its own.

First cut two lengths of grapevine the same size, making sure each end is pointed. These can be about a little longer than one side of the basket rim (this also can vary according to your taste). It is easier in the beginning to be conservative by keeping the ribs smaller. Then cut two more about ½ inch shorter and two more ½ inch shorter than the second two. You should now have three ribs for each side in three different lengths, ½ inch apart. Insert your two largest ones first (one on each side) about midway between the rim and the bottom of the basket (this is where it comes in handy to know where the top is). To do this, bow the vine with one end tucked into the inside of the pocket of the "God's eye" between the rim and the bottom of the handle on the inside. After one side is securely inserted in the God's eye, insert the other end in the other side of the basket. Then insert your next largest side the same way, between the handle and the first rib on each side. Then insert your last two, one on each side between the rim and the last rib inserted. Now you should have a basic shape to start weaving onto with three ribs on each side.

IX-17
Basic frame for egg-shaped basket.

Before you start weaving on the frame, take a minute to sit back, look at your handiwork, and pat yourself on the back. The rest is easy.

To choose your first weaver, try several pieces of the honeysuckle to find the most flexible. Wrap a piece around your hand several times, careful not to bend it sharply. Even though it can be used at this stage, it must be handled gently, slowly winding it around corners instead of forcing it into sharp turns.

When you have chosen a good weaver (two of equal lengths) insert the end at the rim of the basket under the God's eye. Wrap it around the rim and weave under the rib, then over the next, under the next and over the part of the loop which represents the middle rib. It is very important to think of this as a rib also. It makes up the odd rib which makes the weaving come out even. Continue weaving to the other side where the vine is wrapped all the way around the rim of the basket and started back. Continue weaving in this matter until the weaver runs out or you have about an inch or so woven near the God's eye. When you reach the end of the weaver simply tuck the end through the woven vine from the outside to the inside where it will later be clipped when the basket is finished. This should fit neatly against the God's eye in order leaving no open spaces. As you are weaving, push the vines close together with your fingers so that they fit snugly. Now go to the other side and do the same steps there.

IX-18
The beginning of weaving onto the frame.

When you have woven once on each side of the basket, check to see that each section is approximately the same width. At this point you may have to add some to one of the sides to even it up. Even though you measured your weavers to begin with, the vines grow in different widths. Now you are ready to add two more ribs on each side. Hold your basket up to see where the biggest spaces are in the frame. This is where you will want to add the next ribs. Cut two pieces of vine the same size which should be in between the sizes of the two it will be inserted between. Insert a new rib on each side with the pointed end slipped in beside another rib, and pushed in toward the God's eye as far as it will go on one side, with the other end pushed in beside a rib on the opposite side (Photo IX-18). Cut two more to fill in the next two largest spaces. This may sound very haphazard, but it does work and you will find that it is the easiest way to construct a vine basket versus a reed or split basket. This method leaves alot of room to experiment with your basket shape as you work. If you are inclined toward perfection, measure all your ribs in the beginning and insert them in the same manner. I feel part of the enjoyment and excitement of working with vines and other natural materials is experimenting and allowing the vines to create the design by weaving them as they work best instead of forcing them into a preset design.

IX-19
To insert additional ribs, slip a new one in beside an existing one.

Continue weaving from one side to another, inserting one rib on each side at intervals as they are needed, until your ribs are close enough together to make the basket sturdy and the weaving tight. In a medium basket you will have about 5 - 6 ribs on each side. A large one will have more, and a smaller one less, unless you are weaving a small basket with small weavers (such as strawberry runners), or a large basket with extra thick weavers. When you reach the middle and have some space left, where it would not be feasible to weave from one side to another equally, just insert a vine from the inside of the basket to the outside and weave it in until the space is closed. If you find you need help with inserting weavers or weaving closely, you can look around for a sturdy stick and use it as one would use an awl to hold open spaces to insert the vines. This also works for inserting other materials such as bark and decorations.

Now, for the final test...place your basket on the ground and see if it will sit up by itself (no fair placing rocks under it or leaning it against a tree for support). It is does sit up, and you like the way it looks, and if there aren't too many loose ends sticking out, you are a success. For a more finished look, trim the loose ends sticking out. At this point you will really be impressed by the end result you have achieved with just your knife, some vines, patience and creativity.

IX-20
The finished basket.

X

Baskets Made From Vines
and Other Natural Materials

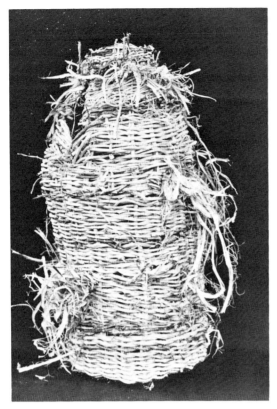

X-1

Honeysuckle and honeysuckle bark basket by
Beryl Lumpkin, approximately 16″ high. The
bark is woven in a swirled motion around the
basket.

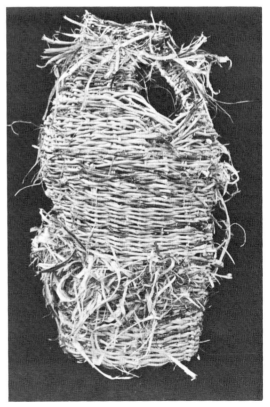

X-2

X-3

PINE NEEDLES: (2″ wide) This basket, created by Jerry Battle from Tampa, Florida, is made from long pine needles, found in many of the southern states. This is an excellent example of a "coiled" basket. The design is created by starting from the center and alternating the stitches as the coils are sewn together.

X-4

MIXED VINES: (12″ wide by 18″ high) This basket, woven by Sherry Hudson of Sneedville, Tennessee, is woven with honeysuckle on a grapevine frame. As you can see, the frame is twisted, which presents a natural design.

X-5

MIXED VINES: by Beryl Lumpkin (12″ wide × 18″ high). The vines in this basket were gathered in Central Florida and were woven when they were freshly cut. If you look closely at the top you can see where the bark began to split as it was worked. The decorations in the center are of dried wisteria and miscellaneous wild vines. They are used merely for decoration and cannot stand alone since they are more brittle than the larger vines.

X-6

HONEYSUCKLE AND CANE: by Beryl Lumpkin (2′ wide × 4′ long). This is one of my favorite baskets and is constructed from many sizes of honeysuckle, old and young. The dark colors on the ends are honeysuckle vines which still have the bark. Honeysuckle bark stripped from the large handles, decorates the end weaving. The large vine which creates part of the handle also creates a design on the bottom of the basket by being woven to the outside (X-8). The cane in the center has been dyed with black walnuts and beechnuts. These dyes give variety to the basket when design is limited, but in this case add to the woven design.

93

X-9

HONEYSUCKLE: (14″ wide × 6″ deep) This honeysuckle basket has been made from honeysuckle which was first boiled, then stripped of its bark. The decorations are from "curled" corn husks. The darker weaving is from vines which were not boiled or stripped. Again, this is a basic "round" basket.

X-10

X-11
By Beryl Lumpkin
This basket is constructed entirely of creek willow. It is approximately **4′** wide × **3′** high.

X-12
"NEST" SCULPTURE
Crossvines, raspberry brambles and mimosa bark with kudzu; twined 20×9×16

X-13
"NESTS" SCULPTURES
Willow and honeysuckle; twined 21×8×15; 12×5×8; 17×6×10

Baskets by Nancy Braski of Oak Ridge, Tennessee. Several natural materials are mixed to create delicate sculpture.

X-14
Pine needle basket by Jerry Battle of Tampa, Florida.

X-15
Virginia Creeper basket (2 ″ × 4 ″) by Beryl Lumpkin, Knoxville, TN.

X-16

Baskets X-16, X-17 and X-18 and photographs by Mary Morrison of Kingston, Tennessee. These baskets are made with a combination of grapevine and reed to achieve unique designs of variations of the egg basket.

X-17

X-18
Basket by Mary Morrison of Kingston. Grapevine, cane and reed.

X-19
Creek willow, honeysuckle and grapevine.
By Beryl Lumpkin

X-20
Bittersweet, honeysuckle and creek willow.
By Beryl Lumpkin

X-21

(6″ wide × 14″ high) This basket was woven with honeysuckle vines and roots. They were used as soon as they were cut with all the bark and roots left on the vines.

X-22
Traditional melon-shaped willow basket. Redbird Mission Crafts, Beverly, KY.

X-23
Mixed vines and moss.

X-24

(2½″ wide × 4½″ high) Honeysuckle which has been boiled and stripped. The top border is hacked over a piece of flat cane.

X-25
Miscellaneous vines have been used for handle and frame in this basket. Woven with cane and trimmed with cedar bark (14″ × 24″).

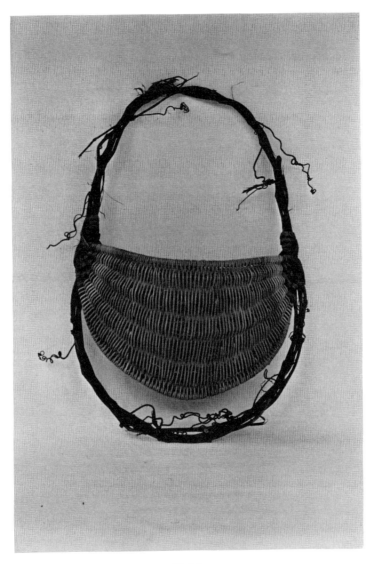

X-26
Grapevine frame woven with reed. Wall basket by Jack Battle, Tampa, Florida.

X-27
Pine needle baskets by Jerry Battle, Tampa, Florida.

X-28
Creek willow (24″ × 30″).

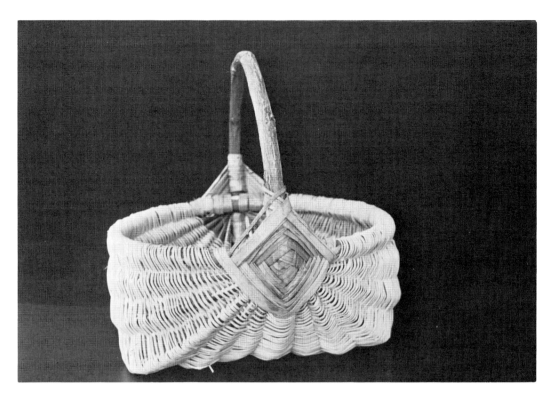

X-29
Traditional honeysuckle basket by Redbird Mission Crafts, Beverly, KY.

X-30
Honeysuckle basket by Jack Battle, Tampa, Florida.

110

X-31

X-32
Baskets by Louise Stod-
dart of Knoxville, TN.
Made from honeysuckle
vines and roots.

X-33

X-34
Baskets by Louise Stod-
dart of Knoxville, TN.
Made from honeysuckle
vines and roots.

X-35
Honeysuckle vines and roots by Beryl Lumpkin.

X-36

X-37
Honeysuckle vines, pine bark, corn husks, pine cones and grapevines by Beryl Lumpkin.

XI

Conclusion

A WORD ON DYING

When making your own dyes, a good rule to follow is that anything you can eat is safe to dye with, such as berries, nuts, grapes, etc. Some materials found in the wild give off toxic fumes and can cause irritation. So, until you know exactly what you are using, dye with caution, and stick to those materials you are familiar with.

If you have any doubts about vines or other natural materials, first make sure they are not poison, then go ahead and try them. You may waste some time in the beginning, but the insight you gain by trying new materials, is well worth the time. You can learn more by the actual trial and error method than you can by reading. You will learn what materials are best for you, and what you enjoy working with most. Some of your best experiences will be the accidental discoveries you make, so don't be afraid to experiment with all types of materials.

The materials mentioned in this handbook are limited, but are intended to give you a guide to begin gathering. I hope you will enjoy gathering and using the materials and methods of weaving I have mentioned, and will find many of your own for very rewarding weaving experiences.

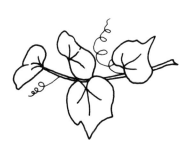